THE SIX DAY BUSINESS

Andrew Speer and Andra Sandru

Copyright © 2018 Andrew Speer and Andra Sandru

All rights reserved.

ISBN: 9781549929908

DEDICATION

To anyone who has had a business idea, but for whatever reason has never pursued it. This one's for you.

CONTENTS

	Acknowledgments	7
1	Day One - Plan and Research	15
2	Day Two - Prototype	25
3	Day Three - Brand Identity	45
4	Day Four - Marketing	55
5	Day Five - Go to Market	67
6	Day Six - Reflection and Next Steps	83

ACKNOWLEDGMENTS

This book would not have been possible without the support from our families and friends who kept pushing us to get this book out there. We also acknowledge the s*** show of a business that we started, without it, we would never have been driven to write this book.

A NOTE FROM THE AUTHORS

Entrepreneurship is extremely difficult (the understatement of the century).

It's stressful.

It's rewarding.

It's not for everyone.

This book is the manual we wish we had when we started our business together in 2015. Looking back we realised there were a number of key questions we could have and should have asked that would have saved us time, heartache, and money that we'd worked long and hard to save.

Even after going through this process we don't have all the answers. What we do have is questions. Questions you need to ask yourself before you dive headlong into your own business.

Our business idea turned out to have a number of critical faults—faults that we did not see because we were blinded by the riches that we would be making in no time at all. Faults that in retrospect (it's always easier in retrospect) we could have identified if we'd asked the right people the right questions.

The Six Day Business is the direct result of what we learned from our experiences.

Our own journey started in 2014 when we met in M60 (a coffee shop in Bucharest—highly recommended!) and immediately started throwing ideas around. Anyone who has experienced this 'high' of idea generation will know that the energy is flowing and you just want to get on with the ideas that you came up with. For us we were talking about making villages from old shipping containers or bags designed with the global traveller in mind.

We both love coming up with ideas and this first meeting was no different.

We settled on an idea fairly quickly—importing and distributing premium eyewear brands into Eastern Europe. We had a good mix of skills (some overlapping) and knew a brand who was looking to break into Eastern Europe.

We were immediately hooked by the margins that distribution provided, we didn't have to manufacture, all—we say all with a grin on our faces now—we had to do was to find retailers.

We went full throttle—buying samples, then stock, forming a legal company and travelling around, without actually stopping and asking a key question—would anyone actually buy these products.

It seems so simple in retrospect.

This is where The Six Day Business would have been invaluable. We would have stopped, reflected, asked the right questions, and discovered the critical flaws not 12 months later when we did figure it out but in the first week.

A good friend of ours once told us that "there's never as much pressure to do something in the moment as you think there is."

We like to think that this sums up the essence of the book. Pause and ask the right questions. You'll thank yourself later.

Every business started somewhere, and that somewhere was not reading and planning. At some point a business actually needs to take a first step.

We will provide you with just enough content to get started—the rest is up to you taking action on the questions that we ask. We want to get you doing, not reading. The Six Day Business could be seen as the prequel to many books on the market right now and you should be confident in the knowledge that even putting your idea down on paper is an important first step.

So...

We want (nay, insist!) you write in this book, add pages to it, and get going. If you run out of space there are pages at the back that you can scribble on.

Finally—before we let you get started, we are very interested in how valuable our readers find this process, so if you do use it, and come to some conclusions (whether you move on with the idea, or not), we'd be very excited to hear about it.

Email us on authors@sixday.business with your successes, failures and tips to make this a better process. We look forward to hearing from you, and including your story in the next book!

Andra and Andrew

IS THIS BOOK FOR YOU?

- You've had a business idea in your head for years and don't know where to start.

- You are overwhelmed because any business book you pick up is 400 pages long and makes you take no action.

- You understand business but don't know where to start with your own idea.

- You are helping/mentoring/coaching/advising people who want to start a business but struggle to take the first step alone.

- You have a relative/friend/partner who keeps talking about their incredible idea but you've never seen any action taken. This book is a polite way of saying "just get on with it."

- You've started businesses in the past and know how much time/energy it can take if you don't ask the right questions at the start.

- You want to try something new.

- Business seems to be something that 'other people' do and you don't think you're able to do it (you are able!).

INTRODUCTION

"An ounce of action is worth a ton of theory"
Friedrich Engels

The Six Day Business is that ounce of action. It's that first step to get you started.

There are literally thousands and thousands of books available to help you grown and scale your business. They're very dense tomes—we're talking 300+ pages of content!

What is usually missing is the action—and action is key. In our minds taking one simple, small concept and applying it with rigour is much more rewarding than being inspired by many great ideas, but not applying any.

The Six Day Business is written by and for aspiring entrepreneurs, for anyone who has a business idea that they want to test. It is a process to help you decide whether you should pursue an idea further.

The beginning of any business is a very exciting time—the temptation can be to drop everything you're doing, invest your life savings, create a 94-page business plan outlining where you'll be in five years and then being shocked when it doesn't work (we've been there).

If you've ever watched Dragon's Den or Shark Tank you'll have seen this time and time again. Through the years there've been many situations where we've thought to ourselves "I really hope this person didn't invest their life savings in this." More times than not they did, and it's tough to watch. This isn't the way to go about it.

We don't want this to happen to you, and as with anything, you need to start from the beginning. We know that you think it's a great idea, otherwise, you wouldn't be here. But who else have you talked to about your idea, or even better, sold a product to?

Don't quit your day-job yet—you owe it to yourself to give yourself every chance to succeed. Think of this as a safe place to test the idea without putting everything on the line.

I know you're keen to get going, but first, spend a few hours with this book over the next six days to form your big idea and take it 'to market' in a simple form. You can complete each step in a few hours a day, and if you're really dying to work on this idea you will be able to fit in before or after work (we would never recommend doing it AT work...). And if you're in-between jobs, then even better, you'll be able to get started quicker!

There will always be a reason (money, family, time) that means it's not the 'right time' to try, but in reality, there's never a perfect moment. Now is the right time. Get started, and see where it will take you. After all, it's not quitting your job—it's testing your idea cheaply and quickly.

These six days will get you closer to making your business a reality. This book is designed to:

1. Give you a step-by-step guide to developing your core idea.
2. Give you the confidence to talk to family, friends, and customers.
3. Help you decide whether it's a good idea, and whether to continue working on it.
4. Help you figure out your next steps if you want to move forward with your great idea.

Let's go!

DAY ONE
PLAN & RESEARCH

"Failing to plan is planning to fail"

Benjamin Franklin... might have said this

//

Day One involves lots of desk based research. For some businesses you will need to get out of the house to look at the local high-street. You will start thinking about the market, potential competitors, your USP and the concepts of supply and demand.

Some questions might warrant more introspection than others—feel free to write as much as you want for each question. It is important to give thought to each question and answer as honestly and comprehensively as you can.

1.1 - WHY DO YOU WANT TO GO THROUGH THIS PROCESS?

There's no one single correct answer to this question.

Maybe you're kept awake at night by your idea. Maybe you want to take the knowledge from your job and apply it to your own business. Maybe this idea is the manifestation of your life's purpose or you've been talking to friends and family about the idea and they've encouraged you to give it a shot. It could be you've spotted a gap in the market and are shocked... shocked that no-one has done it yet. Whatever the reason (and there might be more than one), write it down. Motivations can change, but referencing why you started down this path can keep you motivated in the long-run.

I want to start this business because......

1.2 - WHAT WILL YOUR BUSINESS DO?

Clearly articulating what you do is important. Regardless of who you are speaking to—potential clients, friends, or colleagues—being able to confidently explain why you're different and what you can offer will help spread your message to the right people.

Answering this question might be difficult right now but it will become clearer as we work through the Days.

Imagine you're at a party and somebody asks you what you—and therefore your business—does. Your answer should be clear and concise.

A statement could look like the following:

> I help people with X by doing Y...
> We are the only people in the UK to produce X with Y feature...
> I support X so that Y can happen...
> I am an expert at Y and help other organisations with Z...
> We work with X to increase efficiency of Y and Z...
> Our partners find that X increases 30% when working with us...

1.3 - WHAT BRANDS OR BUSINESSES DO YOU ADMIRE?

Have you ever considered this? Why you like what you like?

Are you 'faithful' to any companies? What do you like about them? Regardless of industry are there brands[1] out there that 'talk to you'. What do you like about them? Is it the imagery, products, innovative spirit, what they stand for, convenience, or is it the or price? Are there any other factors that inspire loyalty for you?

Understanding what appeals to you will help you communicate a compelling message to your customers and also empathise with the factors that influence who they buy from. Below list some brands that you admire and what you admire about them.

I admire....because...

Crossfit — due to simplicity, excellence + reliability. It has changed my life.

Apple — for simplicity.

Dusty Knuckle — for inclusiveness & end product.

---

[1] On www.sixday.business/brands you can find some examples of brands that tell their story very well.

1.4 - WHO ARE YOUR CURRENT COMPETITORS?

Competition is healthy and the aim of this question isn't to deter you. It's to help you understand whether you are entering a crowded market or if you want to carve out a niche. Some competition is good—it can tell you that the market can sustain this type of business.

If there is competition you'll need to ask if it can sustain another one like it. Or are you going to have to entice customers away from their current supplier? Knowing there is fierce competition will force you to think about your positioning, price, and offering to explain why you are different.

Use Google to find competitors and make a list. Use specific search terms to help narrow in on what you are trying to do. If you want to start a restaurant, then your competitors are not only the other restaurants in the area, but also delivery outlets (Deliveroo included) and Netflix (anything that would stop your consumers from leaving their house to come to a restaurant). Think creatively and put down what comes to mind. If you can sell your product globally through e-commerce, then your search will be wider as your competition could be anywhere.

Competitor	Location	Why are they similar	Why will you be different?
Instagram weight business	online	sell weights, gimicky opportunist	quality, we won't be pink goupys. legitimacy
Argos	UK online	we could sell to them?	

1.5 - WHAT IS YOUR UNIQUE SELLING POINT (USP)?

A Unique Selling Point (USP) is any aspect of your business that differentiates it from similar businesses.

You could be unique for a number of reasons including price, quality, location, speed to market or design. The USP could also be you. Just the fact that you are starting the business might be enough to find customers.

Excellent USPs:

Dominos Pizza: You get fresh, hot pizza delivered to your door in 30 minutes or less or it's free.
FedEx: When it absolutely, positively has to be there overnight.
Toms Shoes: We give a new pair of shoes to a child in need for every pair you purchase.

Some businesses spend years figuring out why they are different—we know it's tough. Think of this a hypothesis that you can test in the market. You might think this will make you different, but will it actually? Get something down on paper that you can then iterate and develop as you work through this book.

Our USP will be....

Cheap, high-quality weight product.

- API / sand ordering service? Saw partners

1.6 - WHO IS YOUR IDEAL CUSTOMER?

This is a very powerful visualisation exercise. Describing your target customer—right down to the clothes they wear and the brands they buy—will give you a clearer picture of who you will be selling to. Having this 'perfect customer' in mind will give you useful parameters to consider as you work through price, marketing, positioning, and end-user experience.

Example customer profiles if you are selling direct to businesses:

- Managing Directors of media businesses with between 15 and 30 employees with revenue of over £1.5 million who want to grow to revenue of over £5 million and currently use Oracle for their hosting.

- Human Resource directors who oversee 500+ employees, have budgets of over £300 a year per employee to spend on training, is active on social media (specifically Twitter), and wants to make a quantifiable impact on the organisation.

If you are selling direct to consumers:

- 21-28 year old females who like the brand Toms (because they donate their products), disposable income of over £1,000 per month, work in a major city of over 1 million people, and take public transport to work.

- 30+ year olds who care about how plastic disposal is impacting the planet, spends upwards of £400 a year donating to environmental causes, works in a rural area, and owns two cars.

The more detail the better. Don't leave anything out—you never know what will be relevant later in the process.

As part of your statement, consider the following criteria:

Gender // Age	How do they spend their free time?	Where do they live (city, town, countryside etc.)
Are you targeting certain ethnic groups? If so, who?	What causes do they care about?	What brands do they wear?
Location	What industry do they work in?	What else could be important?
What is the turnover for the business?	Household Income and Disposable Income	Who do they currently buy your service/product/offering from?
	Level of Education	

My ideal customer is...

20+ males who want to workout.
Does: Crossfit, powerlifting, just wants to workout.

Product
- Sand weight
- Water weight
- Sand partners body.

Draw them...

1.7 - WHERE DO YOU SEE A DEMAND FOR THIS PRODUCT?

Demand = consumer's desire and willingness to pay a price for a specific good or service.

Your passion to take an idea to market, and the market's willingness to buy your idea, are two sides of the same coin. Why do you think there will be a demand for your business and what have you seen that supports this? What have you seen that could disprove this?

As irrational human beings we are sometimes thrown off track by what we call 'passion blindness'—in more scientific terms it would be called confirmation bias. Confirmation bias is defined as "the tendency to interpret new evidence as confirmation of one's existing beliefs or theories."

Because you really want this idea to succeed you might discredit information and data that is telling you it's not a great idea. The easiest person to fool is always yourself. When you answer this question try to find evidence that doesn't support what you are trying to do—painful as that might be.

Try to balance your answers between the two columns below. There are rarely ideas that only have one column filled out. Find ways to disprove yourself. They might be stupid ideas and they might not. In Day Five you can discuss these with people you speak to.

Why and where I see demand for this idea.	Factors that indicate there isn't demand.
IG, online, all workout equipment is currently sold out.	Gyms may open up.

1.8 - WHAT IS THE OPPORTUNITY?

Opportunity = all the circumstances and resources that make your business idea most likely to succeed.

Opportunity is finding out why you are in a unique position to take this idea to market. Why are you (and your team—if you have one) the right group that will make this succeed.

Write everything that you believe is relevant to the success of this business and try to stay focussed on what is important to execute on this idea. The more questions you can answer comprehensively, the better you are positioned to pursue this idea. After you work through question 1.9, you may be able to build on these answers to better answer the question, "what is the opportunity?

	Example **Selling Artisanal Tea in a Shop**	**You**
Skills	I get energy from interacting with a wide range of people. Was manager of a tea shop in my home town for 3 years (people management, P&L, basically running small business).	
Expertise	Won UK-wide tea brewing competition Business partner is an expert in tea supply and distribution through his work with a major tea producer.	

Network	Kids go to school in area and have lived here for ten years. Member of community. Know coffee shop owners from other areas that can help with starting up and what to avoid.	
Timing	Local area is getting new infrastructure project which means affluent community moving in.	
Location	Many up and coming areas, like this one, gain popularity and offer great opportunities among new business owners. Young families are moving here and starting businesses. Next year, 22 big retailers are going to open shop in the neighbourhood.	
Other	I have always loved tea and can't start or finish a day without it. Have inherited £4,000, a small portion of which I want to invest in testing this idea.	

1.9 - WHAT COMPLEMENTARY SKILL SETS WOULD BE VALUABLE?

I will reiterate this again—running a business is very difficult. It can be made easier if you have a partner (or partners) that help you along the journey. Not only can they be invaluable with bouncing ideas off of (to make sure you're not going crazy), but they can crucially bring a skill set to the table that you don't possess. You might not currently have anyone in mind for this, but write down what skills/personality traits would be valuable in a partner and then let people know this is the kind of person you want to speak to.

When we started our business we complemented each other—Andrew understood marketing, design and loves numbers, and Andra knows how to start a business, understood the retail industry and has huge amounts of business acumen. Where we didn't complement each other was the fact that we are both ideas people—and sometimes not as strong on execution (especially Andrew–this book has been his biggest project to date!) This wasn't the reason that the business didn't work, and certainly is not insurmountable. It is important to know, and understand, the strengths and weaknesses of who you are working with to make sure you work with those who balance you out.

Your strongest skills	What I am missing

AT THE END OF DAY ONE

Congratulations—you've made it through the first day. It might not seem like much but think about where you were last week, and where you are now. You've taken that first step, and that must feel incredible.

You've discovered what the demand and opportunity could be for your idea, and also found out what your motivations are—both crucial things to know.

We are glad to have you on this journey and look forward to Day Two—when your idea will come to life.

DAY TWO
PROTOTYPE

"As you make a prototype, assume you are right and everyone else is wrong. When you share your prototype, assume you are wrong and everyone else is right."
- Diego Rodriguez Telechea

//

Day Two is where you bring your idea to life. You will need pen and paper, a computer, your full range of creativity, examples of past work and lots of stamina (it's a long day!).

DAY TWO – PROTOTYPE

Day Two is when your idea will move from concept to reality. This step is where most entrepreneurs spend most of their time when starting a business. 'If I build it, they will come' is what we call this mentality—and it's wrong. What you need to do is quickly create and explain an example (prototype) of what you are planning to do, and then effectively communicate this vision to potential customers.

Obviously there are situations where you won't be able to create a full concept in a day—a restaurant comes to mind. However in a day you can create a dummy menu, cook three items from it, write out your story, and then invite a group of friends around to sample the food and hear your positioning. You will need to think laterally and pick key elements of your business—we call these the key features.

We provide many examples below to get you thinking, but we have deliberately left this as one day—a tiny amount of time in the grand scheme of things. This short time span will force you to focus, create a basic example of your idea to then explain to your target market.

The goal of this process is have your potential customers buy-in on the overall concept, and not a finished product. It is true that first impressions are important, however it is just as important to test 'first impressions' with a small group of people to get their feedback and iterate from there.

2.1 - IS YOUR BUSINESS A PRODUCT OR SERVICE?

An idea can come to market in a number of different ways. It is important to know whether you have a product or service based business.

The differences between a product and a service

Product	Service
- Tangible - Fills a need or want for the customer - Takes many forms - Easy to compare quality - Easy to return - Can be kept in stock for a period of time	- Intangible - Heavily based on building trust and a relationship over time. - Takes a single form - Hard to compare quality - Hard to return - It is gone if not sold today

How you can tell whether you're a product or service based business

If we take the example listed in Day One, selling artisanal tea in a cafe, there is more than one way to take artisanal tea to your customers.

Purely Product-Based Artisanal Tea Business	Purely Service-Based Artisanal Tea Business	A combination of Product and Service Business
- Selling bags of tea, tea pots and china in your own shop. - Selling bags of tea wholesale to cafes or to other tea stores.	- Host and run 'How to Make the Perfect Cup of Tea' workshops. - Start a Youtube channel about the best tea and how to brew it.	- Run an artisanal cafe. The service is what your customers will experience in the store, the product is the tea. You could also sell bags of tea in the shop, and run workshops about how to make the perfect cup of tea (a combination of the two above ideas).

My idea is a (product/service/combination)

COST, VALUE, AND PRICE

Understanding the difference between **value** and **cost** will help increase profitability in the long run. The **cost** of your service or product is the amount of money you need to spend to produce it. The **price** is the reward that you receive for providing this service or product. The **value** is the perceived benefit that your customer believes the product or service is worth.

You always want to focus on the value that you can provide, and not on the price that you are charging. Unless you know that you can undercut your competitors significantly, and that your customers are purchasing purely on price, it is a risky strategy to compete on price.

In the next step we will look at discovering what your value is, and then in Day Three we will figure out how to communicate that value. We will come back to pricing at the end of the day.

2.2 - DETERMINING YOUR VALUE

What is the one key feature that you will offer first?

It has been proven that consumers hate choice. Logically we believe that if there is more on offer, more will be sold.

This is wrong and is called the paradox of choice.

The paradox of choice indicates that when there are too many options, people are paralysed by choice, and therefore less likely to purchase anything. As you are testing your idea, choose one key feature or product and focus on providing as much value for your customers through this. As you grow, you will find that more features and products are being asked for—it will be up to you to decide whether there is actually a demand for this, or if would just be a 'nice to have' for your clients.

Your key feature could be based around:

If your key feature is about:	Differentiate yourself by focussing on:	And demonstrate your product like this
Design	Your USP is the way your product or service is designed—frankly people would pay a premium because it looks so good.	Make sure the sketch or materials you take to clients are well designed and show your brand aesthetic.
Quality	The materials you use are the best and this item screams quality—think German design.	Design a high-quality sample or alternatively use imagery that indicates quality and longevity.
Solving a problem	Focussing on the outputs and what the world will be like with your solution.	Show the problem and how you solve it.

Taste	Perfecting your recipe so that with just one bite people will know you're the real deal.	Bake/cook/create the best version of your product. If it's not perfect yet that's ok.
Price	Focus on the huge amount of value you provide for a lower price.	Focus on the huge amount of value you provide for a lower price.
Innovation	You are doing something faster/better/differently.	Show what you have to offer and that it doesn't exist yet.
Quirkiness	You're going against the status quo and want everyone to know this.	Exaggerate the quirk and make sure people know you're different.
Serving a niche	Work only with a small cross-section of customers. Hyper-focus provides a solution that larger firms might not be able to offer.	Be very specific about your target client, and why you want to work with them. Go as far as telling someone that they are not the right client because of X, Y and Z (if it's true).

My key feature is:

2.3 - PRESENTING THE KEY FEATURE OF YOUR IDEA

Now that you've decided on what your key feature is, next you'll focus on how to present it. Remember that you need your clients to understand your key feature, and how you present it will influence how they perceive your product or service.

Examples include:

- **Breadmaker** who loves sourdough. Instead of opening up a shop he focussed on baking the best sourdough loaves and delivering them straight to the consumer. Baked 20 loaves and took them in to the office to share with colleagues.

- **Accountant** who only works with customers in the retail market. Creates a simple one-page website explaining why he is an expert in the retail market.

- **Shoemaker** who uses one material and makes two styles of shoes. Their value proposition is clear—made from a sustainable material and made in a number of colours, it polarises customers (in a good way) who will either identify with the brand, or decide it's not for them.

- **T-Shirt designer** who creates their designs online and then prints out samples using a fulfillment company.

- **Wallpaper Company** that finds niche designs from the 1940s and prints them out on high quality paper. Shows renders of how a room would look with the wallpaper.

- **Designer** can collect examples of current work in one place. Expand previous design work—if they made a logo for a client, they can spend a few hours expanding that to a full brand identity and show what it would look like on a website.

- **Blogger** that writes one chapter from an article themselves and ask a writer friend to also contribute. Create presentation that explains target market, why they are different, and what will be covered on the blog. Come up with a tagline "Like the New Yorker for the German speaking markets."

- **Stationery Brand** that finds high quality paper stock and prints their designs on them. Find envelopes and plastic sleeves and package them in groups of 5 or sold individually.

- **Furniture Refurbisher** who visits eBay and local charity shops to find pieces in need of some restoration. Restore in their own style. Take photos on location in your apartment or house and list online.

Below are more ideas of how to present your idea:

- Images from previous jobs
- Examples of work
- Testimonials
- Samples
- Sketches
- Information you've already sent to family and friends.
- Case studies

I will present my key idea with:

What if I don't have enough to show yet?

In some cases you won't be able to produce enough on this day to comprehensively show what you have to offer.

To add more information to your brand idea you can look back at the list of brands (exercise 1.3) that you admire in day one and look at what appeals from their imagery, products or pricing. From this you can find images on the web that accurately support the brand image you are going for. This could be a stock image, or use complimentary images from other brands that show what you are going for.

You can also use a simple association exercise to help your clients visualise what your idea will be like. Now that you are thinking of starting a business you will hear this everywhere: "I am the uber for dog grooming' or 'I am like the airbnb for hosting events.' These two examples sound ridiculous (they're not far off some of the ideas I've heard though) but use them as a basis to explain your concept. You can also use some of the following terms to quickly communicate look and feel.

- I will use the tone of voice that X uses.
- My brand imagery will be like Y
- My pricing will be less than Z
- I will be in the same bracket of the market as W.
- I'm going to compete against L but be better/faster/better value than them.

What complimentary ideas can you use to explain your idea?

2.4 - HOW TO SET YOUR RETAIL PRICE

Knowing how much money you are making for each unit (either item or time) is key to running a successful business. As with the whole book we are going to boil this day down to its key elements, one of which is knowing how much profit you are making on each item you sell.

It's a simple calculation:

RETAIL PRICE	−	COST OF GOODS (COGS)	=	GROSS PROFIT
The price you're selling your product or service for, or the amount your customer will pay for your product or service.		The cost of your product or service. This includes all the man-hours, and all the resources you use to make your product.		The margin you gain from selling your product.

You will not need to know exactly what your retail price, profit and cost of goods are right now, but having a rough idea when you talk to your potential clients is key.

The **important** thing to remember is that your COGS needs to be lower than your retail price. The larger the gap between COGS and retail price, the more money you'll be making before other operating expenses (salaries, marketing, interest, tax, depreciation, amortisation—which are not covered in this book but are good to be aware of).

Having a retail price in mind when you go to market is important because it will allow you to gauge how you are positioned in relation to your competitors.

When speaking to prospective clients in Day Five you will want to focus on the value that you provide. A commonly used phrase is that 'cost is only an issue in the absence of value.' However we also know that when you first start talking about your idea it will be tough to completely describe your value to a point where someone doesn't care about the price. We want you to focus on the value, but if (and it's a good sign) that someone asks about the cost, we want you to be ready.

PRICING FOR SERVICES

We are going to cover two of the common ways to charge for a service: hourly rate, and project-based.

Hourly Rate

There is a very exact calculation (that differs from person-to-person) about how much to charge for a service. It takes into account all of your overheads, what profit you want, and other factors[2]. This is something that we recommend doing when this process is done.

To figure out an estimate of an hourly rate you can do some desk research. Look online for similar businesses and see what they charge. When Andrew first started freelancing he found it very uncomfortable to ask for his hourly rate, but once he took in to account salaries, expenses, insurance and everything else that comes along as part of running a business, he became more comfortable with it, and even raised his prices.

At first it will probably be uncomfortable asking for your hourly rate but as your confidence in yourself, and your business rises, you'll be able to charge more and more.

Project-Based Rate

When we use the word project we mean anything from a six month consulting gig to cutting someone's hair. It is one cost in exchange for something. There are two main way to price a project. The first is to take whatever hourly rate you have come up with, multiply it by how long you think it will take, and build in 10% for a either a profit margin or room to negotiate with your client. ugh costing. . When charging by the project you need to be very clear about the deliverables, how many revisions you will make, timelines and any other factors that could make the project take longer than anticipated. Again, as you work on more projects you will get better at figuring this out.

This won't be your final pricing structure but having a figure in mind when speaking to a potential customer will make you look prepared.

Pricing for Products

Unless you are playing in a completely new niche, there should be other businesses on the market that have similar offerings. Go back to your list of competitors and do some desk research—how much are they charging for what

---

[2] More details on www.sixday.business/hourly-rate

they do. It is up to you to determine whether you should charge more, or less. Remind yourself of the difference between value and price. Don't undervalue what you are offering, but also be aware that you can raise your prices at a later date, and as we are in a testing phase, nothing is final.

I will charge..

2.5 - HOW WILL YOUR CUSTOMERS BUY FROM YOU?

There are different ways to charge a customer for what you offer. It is important to articulate the how people can buy from you.

If we take the example of the **breadmaker** and **the lawyer** then there are a number of ways that they can sell their products and services.

	Breadmaker	**Lawyer**
Individual Sales or project-based work	Selling loaves of bread directly to a customer. This could be through a market stall, setting up a shop or selling online.	Offer a fixed cost service for 'bread and butter' work (wills, divorces, estates).
Subscription or Retainer	Set up a monthly service where one loaf of bread is delivered each week. Helps retention because you have confirmed revenue each month and allows you to forecast	Pay X amount each month and have access to a set amount of legal advice or hours each month. Roll it over if someone doesn't use all their minutes at once.

My customers will buy from me by:

2.6 - FURTHER QUESTIONS

It would also help if you can answer the following questions (not essential but helpful!)

What problem does your idea solve?

Why should people work with you?

Why should anyone care that you are starting a business?

AT THE END OF DAY TWO

This day is exhausting for most people—you're not alone. It has (hopefully) forced you to think about tangible ways to present and show your idea to potential customers. It might not seem like you have enough for 'a business,' but being a) very clear about what your initial offering is and b) being able to display it in a way that makes sense to your customer, is an incredibly powerful way to start.

In Day Three we will look at brand identity—creating a name and logo for your business.

DAY THREE
BRAND IDENTITY

"A brand is a reason to choose"

Cheryl Burgess

//

Day Three is when you create your first brand for your business. Don't worry if you're not creative, we have some hints and tricks to get you through this.

DAY THREE – BRAND IDENTITY

I'm wearing a...
I just bought a...
I only work with...
I need another...

Just reading through the list above I'm sure names came to mind.

A brand identity is how your target consumer views your business. A number of elements make up a brand: logo, name, tagline, typeface, and tone of voice. Together these indicate the value that your business will bring to the consumer.

Each of these elements is important, but for today we are going to focus our attention on the name and logo.

3.1 - CREATING A NAME

The name is one of the first things a customer will hear about you. This makes it important, and this is why many people get stuck trying to find the perfect name—trust us, in the past we've taken weeks to come up with a name. We don't want you to overthink this. The name needs to mean something to you—after all, you'll be seeing it the most! You can easily develop both the name (and an eventual tagline) once you have a better idea where you want your company to go.

Key points when choosing a name:

- Memorable, easy to pronounce and specific.
- Not taken by another company—search on Google or local business agency[3] to see if it already exists.
- Check Godaddy.com to see if the URL is available. Even though you won't be setting up a website at this point it is good to check. You might find a competitor with the same name—that wouldn't be good!
- As a bonus—it helps if it's not so complicated that you have to explain the thought process behind it

---

[3] http://beta.companieshouse.gov.uk for the UK

If you're struggling to think of something, look at a Thesaurus (did an episode of Friends come to mind? No? Nevermind), and find synonyms for words that resonate with your brand. You can even think about a play on words, or even an anagram.

Through the years we have named businesses after pets, streets and randomly chosen words from the dictionary. Right now we have a business named for Andrew's Grandpa's middle name, a stylised version of the word 'curator' and something called Small Blank Books, because well, the first books were small... and blank.

Sometimes we have spent more time on the name than the business and needless to say, not all of these businesses still exist. Use this table to jot down any words that come to mind when you think about your business. This is a great brainstorming exercise to align the name you choose with your goal as a business.

Words that resonate with you or stand for something relevant to your business.	
Terms that define your business	
Descriptive and unique selling points of your business	

Personal details about the founder(s)	
Example of brands that you think are best described by their name.	
Your ideas for names	
Chosen name and tagline	

Try it now—"Hi I'm X and I run _____". How does it sound, how does it feel?

3.2 - DESIGNING A LOGO

After driving for hours, you see a golden arch that gets larger and larger. You start to feel hungry without realising it. You know what it stands for, even though you didn't read the full name. You didn't need to.

At the most basic level a logo is a combination of text and images to help us identify different brands. Right now a logo will help you look established and eventually it could mean so much more—it can be the foundation of your whole brand and will help your customers relate to what you value, what you do and who you are. To portray all of this in an image can seem like a big responsibility.

If you are struggling for inspiration you could use a service like Pinterest.com to spark your creativity and give you some ideas.

Let's Talk Symbols And Colours

Colours

Colours can create strong associations with different moods. According to studies, some colours are associated with anxiety, others are known to induce calmness.

Knowing the basics can help you decide what associations you want for your brand.

- **Blue** is the colour of sky and sea and is often associated with depth, stability, trust, loyalty, wisdom, confidence, intelligence, faith and truth.

- **Red** is the colour of fire and blood, so it is associated with energy, war, danger, strength, power, determination.

- **Green** is the colour of life, renewal, nature, and energy is associated with growth, harmony, freshness, safety, and environment and is also associated with money, finances, banking, ambition, greed and jealousy.

- **Yellow** is the colour of joy, happiness, intellect, and energy and produces a warming effect, arouses cheerfulness and stimulates mental activity.

- **Black** is the colour of power, seriousness and strength and indicates prestige and elegance.

- **White** is the colour of goodness, purity and light and is considered to be the colour of perfection.

Symbols

A similar principle applies when determining the meaning of different shapes:

- **Circles** show unity and friendship.
- **Straight edges** show practicality and stability.
- **Triangles** show power.

For stories behind the most recognisable logos in the world search "most recognisable logos of all time" online. There are some fascinating stories out there for those who love branding!

Now it's your turn:

Colours that you want to represent your business:

Shapes and imagery that are relevant to your business, the tools needed to perform it, or the selling point.

Brands that you think have great logos. Why do you think they're great? It could be design, colours, style, etc.

Your turn to draw! Combine shapes with your chosen name and keep going until you feel like you're getting closer to something you you like (when money is coming in you can develop it further). This section will definitely not be big enough for everyone—get some pieces of paper (or use the blank space at the end of the book) and draw, draw, draw.

3.3 - NEED HELP DESIGNING THE FINAL LOGO?

It is important to have a logo because you will want to use your logo in the marketing you create and then again when you ask for feedback on your idea in Day Five.

If creativity isn't your cup of tea you can find a freelancer online[4] and have a logo made quickly, easily, and cheaply. You will be able to find freelancers that will work with your ideas and come back with a simple logo within a day or two, for the price of a few coffees.

To help the designer you should send them the drawings you've created (you can take a photo of the pages) plus examples of logos and brands that you like. When working with someone for the first time try to be as clear as possible with what you want. This will save time and money and help the designer understand what you are after.

As with anything, you are going to get what you pay for so don't expect Michelangelo on a shoestring. If you decide to take this business further you can spend more to get a professional brand made for you.

Editor's Note: All these small expenditures will add up, so if you decide to continue with this business you will want to keep all expenses as low as possible. For the first few years this logo might work fine!

---

[4] Fiverr, Freelancer.com, Upwork, Guru or Peoplehour

AT THE END OF DAY THREE

Finishing Day Three means you now have an idea of what your business will do, an awareness of competitors, have an initial prototype and a brand! Day Four will be testing your creativity further by diving deeper in to marketing.

DAY FOUR
MARKETING

"Advertising is the price you pay for being unremarkable."
- Jeff Bezos

//

Day Four is where you learn about marketing, and how it can make or break even the best businesses. We will explain in more detail about what a USP is, and how to craft your own.

DAY FOUR – MARKETING

Marketing is the process of educating consumers why they should choose your product or service over your competitors. It's a simple definition, but crucial to the ongoing success of your business.

The goal of Day Four isn't to create a complete marketing solution for your business. Instead it is to:

1. Find out who else is in the market who does a similar thing (market research).

2. Determine your Unique Selling Point (USP).

3. Choose one online platform to display information about your business.

4. Create content to explain your USP on your chosen platform.

This is our last day before we take your idea to market. We will build on ideas from previous days and refine further exactly what your business will be offering.

4.1 - MARKET RESEARCH (INDUSTRY OVERVIEW)

Market research is finding gathering information about the market environment and what consumers want and need.

For every industry and product sector there are endless books and reports available. There is the danger of going down a rabbit hole with reading and research. Set yourself an hour or two to spend on this—you can always come back to it later and research in more depth.

	Examples	**Your Business**
What industry are you in?	Technology/Telecommunications Professional/Business Services Manufacturing Real Estate Food and Beverage Retail Healthcare Non-profit or Other	
Is their growth in your industry in the area where you will be selling?	Yes, my target audience increased their expenditure on sweet goods from £3 per week per person to £5 per week per person between 2010 and 2018.	
Where will you be selling?	On the high-street near the local train station	

What is the opportunity where you will be selling	Affluent middle-class neighbourhood with high level of 'cafe culture.'	
Do you have many competitors in your marketplace?	Yes—there are 2 cake shops plus 3 coffee shops that sell cakes.	

From what you've read about the market, what are you thinking? Have you found a niche? Is the market saturated? Is there a company doing something similar?

4.2 - DETERMINING YOUR USP—WHY ARE YOU DIFFERENT?

Now we need to determine what makes you different—your USP. In Day One we quickly jotted down what you thought your USP is. Working through the previous three days should have given you more insight in to what makes you different.

	Copywriting and marketing for lawyers	**Your Business**
Core Function	Provide accurate, well written articles and blogs for law firms.	

Take a moment and review what you have written so far. Looking back at all three days will help you complete this stage. We want to communicate what makes you different in the market place, and why a customer would choose you over a competitor. Function, benefits and features are good starting points to find out what makes you different.

Benefits (What you want to communicate)	Accuracy is a given—everything I do is 100% checked and accurate. Researcher on the team who has a law background. Only work with lawyers so I know what is happening in the industry.	
Features (important to know but not what you want to communicate).	Quick—I can turn around articles within 48 hours, essential for a fast-moving industry. Confidentiality.	
Looking at your features, how would you describe why you are different?	Copywriting for the agile, fast-moving law firm.	

4.3 - WHERE SHOULD YOU COMMUNICATE WITH YOUR CUSTOMERS?

Next we need to decide how to package and present the features and benefits of your idea. In some cases great marketing can be more important than a great product.

Before you strive to have a Super Bowl Halftime slot, you might want to start with social media—it's cheap and easy to get started. If used well social media can be 'oxygen' for any startup. It's one of the best tools available for individuals and companies to put content in front of a wide audience. There are a few general things that can help you tremendously. In the market research section you would have seen your competitor's online presence. What stood out? What would you like to replicate?

What stood out?	I immediately knew who Articles4Accountants clients were… I knew how to get in touch with them quickly…
What would you like to replicate?	The story that they told really made me resonate with them…
Social Media accounts that have great content	

4.4 - CHOOSING A PLATFORM

After looking at accounts you like, it is time to choose one to post information about your business for potential customers. This is where you will direct potential customers in Day Five so that they can find out more about what you do.

There are a number of platforms out there where you can post content: below is a table with some examples and when to use each of them.

Works for most industries	Not for everyone
Facebook Page: Small text bio with images, videos and posts **Instagram:** Images and videos **Medium.com:** Long form articles with images. **Twitter:** Text (under 280 characters), images, videos. **Linkedin:** Blog articles, videos.	**Soundcloud:** Audio recordings for musicians or DJs. **Behance:** Portfolio for designers, illustrators and artists. **Youtube:** Videos for vloggers (video bloggers) and videographers.

The most prolific accounts provide a steady stream of content, and have a recognisable style. You don't need to post constantly but it's a great opportunity to communicate what makes you different in a cost effective way.

This will be especially important if you decide to continue on with your idea when you are finished working through this book. If your customers expect you to deliver a consistent message online, then it is up to you to continue to do this. You may also decide that the best way to get customers is through referrals. If so, focus your attention there.

However you decide to take your idea to market, it is important to have some sort of online presence so that people can find out more about what you do.

I will use _____ to show my business to potential customers.

4.5 - CREATING CONTENT

Now that you have chosen a platform to present yourself to the market you will need to choose what type of content you will need to create. Look back at Day Two—what elements did you create in Day Two that can be easily posted online?

There are a number of ways to demonstrate what you do:

- Posting **images** of your products/services.
- Sharing **videos** that introduce key parts of your business.
- **Blogging** about why you are different.
- Sharing other **brand images** to create the 'look and feel' of your business.
- Recording your **music** to share.
- **Writing** a brand manifesto.

Try to answer the question: "After I tell someone about my business, where can they find out more?"

I will _____ and post it on _____ to _____

Write an article	Instagram	show why I'm different
Take photos	Twitter	explain my prototype
Record a video	Facebook	introduce my business to customers

You don't have to stay with just one channel, but you want to put something somewhere for potential customers to visit after you have spoken to them.

4.6 - BARTERING

Bartering is exchanging goods or services without using money.

Bartering is incredibly useful in any early stage of a business. There are many services that you and your business can offer, in exchange for the services of others.

Most startups are not backed-up by limitless supplies of cash. Being smart about how you spend the money you have saved to start, and then initial cash flow, is crucial. You would be surprised how many services you can offer someone—both relevant to the business and otherwise.

Start by making a list of **what you can offer** a business or individual:

Examples	Your Business
Make orders for "free"	
Make other items not in your offering	
Photoshop and retouch photos	
Build a website and upload products	
Introduce someone to somebody in my network	
Give out a "fidelity card" into your future business with freebies or discounts	
Hold a baking class for a small group	
Run errands and deliver groceries	
Offer to serve as a sales person at an event or pop-up	
Takeover a group activity or a chore for a preset time	
Do an activity I would do anyway for my business, but doing it for somebody else too	

Example	What you need	Who do you know who might be open to a barter
Promotion for my business- blogger, influential, another business etc.		
A customer database (relevant to me) from someone who targets the same clients, but not a competitor.		
Take photos of my business to post on social media channels.		
The name of a supplier or to help me with my manufacturing/ development process.		
Somewhere to store my first manufacturing run.		
An introduction to somebody in their network.		
Entrance to an event.		
Give feedback and test my business.		

Reach out to five of these people now and ask for what you want. Remember to explain what you can do for them.

AT THE END OF DAY FOUR

Day Four was about thinking, and then formulating how you present what you do. Now when someone asks "what does your business do" you'll be able to answer concisely to explain who you are, what you do, and why you are different.

This will be key tomorrow so make sure that you can answer those questions fluently and with conviction.

DAY FIVE
GO TO MARKET

"Price is only the issue in the absence of value."

Anon

//

Day Five is the most challenging of all the days. It is very fun to sit behind a computer screen making a business, it's a whole 'nother kettle of fish when you take it out to the world and speak to people about it. It's tough, but it has to be done sooner or later. This is sooner, and the faster you get can get used to talking to people about your idea, the better you will become at doing it.

DAY FIVE – GO TO MARKET

Until now the idea has been in your head and in the pages of this book. Now it's time to get feedback from 'the market' to see what people think.

Day Five is about finding the right people to talk to, and most importantly, asking the right questions. We asked the wrong questions to the wrong people when we started our business, and we suffered considerably because of it.

5.1 - WHAT ARE THE RIGHT QUESTIONS TO ASK?

We cannot stress the importance of this section enough.

We've found that many questions about a business are linked to a future state that may or may not happen. We were certainly guilty of this.

What we should have done differently

Before you dive in to your own questions, we want to share some of the key questions that we failed to ask, and the answers that we would have received.

>Q: "Is there a need in the market for this"
>
>A: "Even though the Eastern European market for niche of luxury products is growing, unknown brands, that have no previous track record, no marketing, no proprietary features, might not be an immediate choice for somebody that wants to make a purchase"
>
>Q: "How big is the market?"
>
>A: "In Romania, there are 3 big retail chains that sell sunglasses and eyewear and they make up 95% of the market (e.g. if you don't crack a big retailer in Romania you're going to struggle."
>
>Q: "How likely are you to put this brand/product in your store"
>
>A: "The optical market and retailers are 90% supplied by two of the biggest companies in the world:

Luxottica and Safilo. Combined, the two own most of the sunglasses and eyewear brands in the world. The other 10%, retailers buy unbranded "white label" frames, that are significantly cheaper than any branded products. The idea that retailers would give up shelf space to a brand that is unknown, with no star power behind it, is not really competitive with the margins they get from the other customers, with no history in return rates and quality checks, with not a lot of money to offer as "incentives", is incredibly unlikely."

We could have easily asked the three questions above in the first week (even through desk based research) and it would have given us an accurate view of the market and would have saved us 11 months and £43,000.

Asking the right questions

If you ask a friend if they will come to your store when it opens the answer will probably be "of course". This could be because they are a friend and want to be polite, or it might mean that they shop at this kind of store all the time and will move their loyalties to you. However from this type of questions you have no idea which is true and cannot take this answer at face value as intent to purchase.

It is crucial to anchor your questions to activities and behaviours that have already happened in the past—past behaviour is the best predictor of future behaviour. You want to talk about their life specifically instead of in generics and after you ask the question you want to listen, and not interrupt.

It is good to have a list of questions that you want to ask, but because you always be listening you will be able to hone in on answers that will provide further answer to prove or disprove your idea. If we take one of the examples below:

> If you ask "when was the last time you went to a cupcake store" and the answer is "the day before my son's birthday," instead of moving on to the next question you will want to probe with some follow-up questions because it might be that they only go to a cupcake store to get cupcakes for birthdays and not as an everyday occurrence. If you take it at face value of 'yes they go to cupcake stores' you might be missing the point.

This can be the most difficult part of this process—asking the right questions. Make sure you have a list (that you can alter) and keep track of any follow-up questions you ask as they might become more valuable than the original list you have written out.

Good Question	Bad Question
When was the last time you went to a cupcake store?	Will you come to my cupcake store when it opens?
In the last month how many loaves of bread have you purchased?	Do you buy lots of cupcakes?
On the weekend would you seek out something sweet, like pastry or cake?	What is your favourite type of cupcake?
(If they have family) What causes your children to stop and say they want one of those?	Do you use Amazon?
Have you tried anything else?	
How are you dealing with it now?	
What else should I be asking you?	

Watch out for the fluff

In Rob Fitz's book The Mom Test[5] (which is on our recommended reading) he says that you need to watch out for positive fluff. Because we are the easiest people to fool when we hear 'oh that's a great idea,' it plays straight to our ego and we then leave thinking we have some support for our business.

Sticking to quantifiable questions that are anchored to the past will allow you to cut through the fluff and get valuable information. Don't be afraid to probe deeper about why someone has answered the way they have. It is much better to have an uncomfortable conversation now and get valuable information that will initially be disappointing but will save you time down the line.

When we started our business in Romania we asked lots of ego based questions. We asked the questions to people

---

[5] www.sixday.business/mom-test

who really had no vested interest in the success or failure of our personal business. They wanted their own business to succeed (which would be helped by our success), but it wouldn't be the end of the world if it didn't. We represented a brand who we bought products from before attempting to resell them to high-street retailers across Romania. For our partner, Eastern Europe wasn't a priority market, so any success we had selling the products was a bonus.

Without stepping back and thinking about their vested interest in our success, I studiously created a beautiful business plan that was based on no more than ideas I came up in my head. The furthest we went to validate the idea was asking our contact at the brand whether it was possible to sell this amount month-to-month (from my fake plan). They said "yes, of course".

If I'd taken time to step back and ask myself if this person was a) a believable person (they have the experience and knowledge to be reliable on this subject in this geography) and b) if there is any reason this person would tell me it was a good idea even if it isn't, then we would have had a strong reason to doubt what they were telling us.

5.2 - WHO SHOULD YOU ASK?

Finding the right people to talk to is crucial. The first people that buy your product are most likely to be people you know directly or through people you know. You want to find potential customers, or those that you believe will give useful, relevant and reliable feedback.

First we are going to look at the people who you already know that will be willing to give you feedback.

Make a list of your three biggest fans, people that support you in whatever you do:

1.
2.
3.

Who always tell you exactly what they think, even if it isn't always supportive? These people are essential to have in your life, and if you don't have them, find some.

1.
2.
3.

Who do you know in the industry that you are trying to enter? Even if the link is weak, it wouldn't hurt to ask them for 10 minutes of their time.

1.
2.
3.

These are the nine people you should speak to. They will give a range of answer could be positive, full of fluff, or even critical (you need critical!)

Regardless of who you talk to, if you really value their advice you should ask them to give frank, candid feedback, regardless of if it is negative. Negative feedback is just as valuable at this stage. If you come away with nine answers of "this is the best idea ever" then a) you have the best idea ever (unlikely) or b) people are not giving you their true opinions because they are worried about hurting your feelings (more likely).

Take every piece of feedback with a grain of salt

There are two ways to make sure you are being critical about the feedback you get:

1. Make sure to get a wide range of opinions (split between critical and positive feedback) and make sure to determine whether they are a target customer or not. This will allow you to gauge the value of their feedback. A simple way to do this is rank their value as a consumer. If someone is wildly positive about your idea, but has bought one cupcake in 10 years, it may seem like good feedback but it probably isn't worth

much. On the flip side if you have a cupcake connoisseur saying that the recipe is wrong, it is more valuable but also it might not just be to their taste. Use your judgement.

2. Not all feedback is created equal. Look through this list of nine people and give them a ranking from one-nine to indicate whose feedback you will take the most seriously. If you have picked a strong list of nine this exercise will be tough. If you find it is easy to put someone at the bottom of the list it might be worth replacing this person with someone else.

If you could talk to the 'perfect' person about your business, who would it be?

This person might not exist in your network right now, but let people know that you are looking to speak to them and you'd be amazed at what manifests itself. For us, as we are writing The Six Day Business, we would like to talk to someone who has worked in the publishing industry for 30 years, has written and published six books, knows publishers and is also an agent (if anyone knows this person let us know!)

The perfect person to talk to is

WHERE TO FIND FEEDBACK

You already have a list of people to speak to—but what if you want to get more feedback?

Ask Family and Friends for Recommendations

Family and friends are a great starting point, because they want to see you succeed and will generally help wherever possible.

On the flip side, family and friends are most likely to give you biased advice, as they don't want to hurt your feelings. You can frame the conversation well at the beginning using phrases like:

> "I know you love everything I do, but I really want your feedback as a consumer, not as my mother!"

This group will be the most subjective group to toughest to be objective with because you know them the best. Remember to rank their opinions as you would anyone else's.

People in your wider network

When you start talking about your idea to family and friends, inevitably they will say:

> "Oh you should talk to X, they are in this industry."

Ask for recommendations and give the 'recommender' an outline of what you want to ask:

> "I am testing out different business ideas and want to talk to someone in X field. I would love to set up a quick call (no more than 15 minutes) to hear your honest views on what I am planning on doing".

Once you put your ideas out to the market you will be surprised that Uncle Steve's third cousin's brother runs the largest X business in the area. This happens all the time so make sure to tell people what you are planning on doing.

People that my network know:

Speaking to potential customers at local events

If your prototype is at a stage where someone could buy it, then you need to put yourself in a position to sell it.

You have your logo, you have your marketing material, and for a few hundred pounds more you can apply to have a stand at a local market/fair/event.

Do some desk research to find somewhere to start. Search 'local markets in X town' to find places in your area. You could use more specific terms—'local food markets' (if you're selling food) as it might be worth going further afield if it means talking to the right people.

You won't be able to find and set up at a market in one day, but keep this in mind as an option as you continue to test your idea.

I remember the first time we went to a market—it was exhilarating and nerve wracking in equal measures. We were selling our accessories brand uju & co. (the name was taken from the Zulu word for honey—don't ask). I still remember that moment when the first product was sold—it was exhilarating and validating at the same time. Those first customers could turn in to your biggest fans. Get their details and ask if you can stay in touch.

It was also very humbling as hundreds of people walked by and didn't purchase what we'd made. It was tough for our ego. It's a fact of business that there will be lots of rejection—don't take it personally (easier said than done) and use it as a learning experience at every stage.

Any time you have an opportunity to ask someone for feedback, take it—the idea is always to to talk to as many potential customers as possible and get their feedback.

If they buy, great, ask them what appeals. If they're interested but don't end up buying anything, ask (kindly) what swayed them to not make this purchase. Write down your observations studiously and gather as much information as possible. Use this experience to ask a range of questions (building on the work you did in exercise 5.1) and try to get as many views as possible.

If one person says "nope, I would never pay £6 for a cupcake," it might just be a one-off. However if no-one buys all day, and you hear that feedback seven times, than that is very useful.

If you do decide to continue with your idea, markets are a great way to start to build brand presence, community, and awareness. They are also normally run on the weekend, so you can test your ideas without quitting your day-job, meet other small business owners, and build up a network to support you. The experience that those around you have gathered will help you progress faster than if you sat behind a computer all day.

One last thing to mention about market stalls is to pay attention to the costs. For this initial test it is OK making a loss if you are getting key feedback. If you are planning to do this each weekend, and the stall costs £180, the car rental costs £40, and the cost of making the cupcakes (plus your time) comes to £74 than you know that you have to sell £294 worth of cupcakes just to break even.

Even though you might not breakeven the first time, if you're asking the right questions then it is worth the money.

Markets I could sell at:

Social Media Contacts

If you've spent any amount of time on social media over the years you will have built up a network with like-minded people. Now is the time to leverage those contacts. LinkedIn can be particularly valuable, as it's main purpose is professional networking. Your connections on LinkedIn can be a valuable source of feedback. It is worth looking at who you follow on Twitter and Instagram to see if there is anyone you can connect with and start to build up a relationship.

If you have connected with someone (whether you know them or not), they have given you permission to contact them, and that's what you should do. If you don't know them well you can send the following message, personalised based on what you know about them and their expertise:

> Dear X,
>
> We have been connected on Linkedin/Twitter/Instagram for a while and I have enjoyed your contributions.
>
> I am thinking of doing X, and because of your experience in Y, I would love to ask you a few questions to understand your views.
>
> Would you be free for a ten minute phone call this week? Let me know what works for you.
>
> Regards,
>
> Andrew

It's straightforward, to the point, and makes a clear ask. You probably won't hear back from the majority of people, but again, make a list of ten people, send the message, and see what happens. You'd be absolutely amazed at what people are willing to share if you approach the conversation from a perspective of pure curiosity.

Online or Physical Resellers

Finding a direct path to your customers, through either a physical retailer or online store, is another route to go straight to market. There are benefits to working with people who already have foot traffic (either with brick and mortar, or an online shop) you can then leverage. The margins (how much gross profit you make on each item) will be lower when you do this (as you will have to account for the retailer needing to make money as well), but if you are providing a great product, and they have customers, it can be a match made in heaven..

'Cold calling' on a retailer made us nervous when we first did it (and still does) but it's a quick route to honest and productive feedback. If you're polite, friendly and straightforward you'll be amazed at how willing people are to talk to you.

Keep in mind that these retailers (if they stock a number of brands) make money by finding cool, useful, or valuable products that their customers are going to buy. If your product fits this category than you have a chance at being stocked.

Try to approach stores when they are likely to be less busy. This will make it easier to build a rapport with staff.

Sometimes you might get answers that seem positive, but really are not helpful:

> If a retailer says "this is nice, let me know when you launch"
> You might think "YES! A retailer really wants to buy my products".

In reality they didn't say they want to buy your product. They said that they would like to know more information in the future. No commitment to buy, no feedback on the product, and no real valuable information.

At this point the temptation is to leave with a boosted ego. Instead, it is the time to dig in more specifically. Think back to section 5.1 - 'what are the right questions to ask' and use some of the below questions to dig in on what they say.

- How many of X product do you sell in a year?
- When was the last time you sold one?
- Do you have room for another X in your store?
- Who else would I need to talk to make a decision?
- Would you be willing to pre-order five units to get a good price? I know your customers will love them.[6]

As with all of these questions, you will get better as you go along and gain more confidence to talk about what you do.

---

[6] For more information on how to sell we recommend "Exactly How to Sell" by Phil M. Jones. Visit www.sixday.business/exactly-sell to find out more.

When we first approached retailers to buy our watches and sunglasses we made the mistake of taking answers at face value when there was no commitment to buy. We left a 90 minute meeting feeling like we'd made a big sale, when in reality the only thing that happened was at the end of the meeting they said *"I like the design of the glasses, send over the lookbook and then we will touch base"*.

In reality after calling this person 15 times over the next few months we never made one sale to this retailer. This tiny bit of ego-boosting feedback made us continue down this path for a few more months. It's amazing what you can miss when you hear what you want to hear.

If we'd asked better questions, and looked at what the motivations were for this retailer (they worked with one main brand and needed a huge amount of stock to move forward—something we couldn't provide).

It's uncomfortable for most people to do this (and if it isn't, lucky you!) but it's the fastest way to get to market, and get great information.

Shops that I can approach....

One last thing

Practice makes perfect. This section might take longer than a day, but it is also something that you should never stop doing as you move forward with your idea.

You'll find many people want to help, give advice, and tell you what they would love to see with your idea. This is great, they're engaged. However, even if you do make what they suggest, it probably doesn't mean they will buy it, only that they think it would be cool. Keep an eye out for 'feature creep,' which you can normally tell is happening when someone says "if you do this, I might consider it." In most cases they won't. Your idea has a market—stick to it, be specific about what you offer, and you'll find your people.

Remember

- Trust your gut. If what you are hearing is completely contradictory to what you are seeing in the market, then analyse where the discrepancies are, and come to your own conclusion. If it feels like bad advice/feedback then ask yourself "why don't I think this is true?" and try to be as analytic as possible.

- Always tell people where they can find out more (the online presence you set up in Day Four).

- Ask for email addresses from everyone so that you can keep them in the loop, and potentially ask more questions as you develop your business.

AT THE END OF DAY FIVE

Another full day. You probably have conversations, questions, and suggestions swirling around your head—and that's good. The day is meant to give you lots of information. In Day Six we will help separate the wheat from the chaff and see what advice is worth taking onboard, what needs to be discarded, and importantly, whether it is worth spending another Six Days, Six Months or Six Years on this idea.

•

DAY SIX
REFLECTION AND NEXT STEPS

"Give me six hours to chop down a tree and I will spend the first four sharpening the axe."

- Abraham Lincoln

//

Where Day Five was asking opinions of others, Day Six is about asking yourself some tough questions. Find a quiet spot where you're not going to be disturbed, turn off your phone, and lean into the (what could be uncomfortable) process.

This day might take longer than the others as you let the ideas percolate, gain more inspration and rest. But do it propertly.

DAY SIX – REFLECTION AND NEXT STEPS

You started from an idea, brought it to life, learnt about marketing, created a brand identity, and then took your product to the market.

After the chaos of the first five days, Day Six is a day of reflection. It is a day to look (as objectively as possible) at whether you came up with an idea that is worth spending more time on. We have given you the process to build out your idea, and ask the right questions. It is now time for you to make the choice that is right for you.

These questions are designed to really make you think. I've used this line before, and I'll use it again.

> "The first principle is that you must not fool yourself—and you are the easiest person to fool."
> - Richard Feynman

This is not a test, no-one is going to look at your answers. Being brutally honest with yourself is difficult but incredibly rewarding. The questions are designed to make you realise what the next steps are, and whether you've come up with a great idea! After you've worked through the questions you could bounce your answers off the trusted confidants you talked to in Day Five. Ask them to dive in to your answers and challenge your assumptions.

Remember—you are the one who will have to drive this idea forward day-by-day. Are you willing to do that?

6.1 - LOOKING BACK

We will start by looking back at the last five days.

What was your biggest takeaway?	
What surprised you?	

What are the first thoughts that come to mind about this process?	
Who else should you have talked to?	
What have you learnt?	
What was the most challenging part (this can help you determine where you might need to look for complementary skill sets from a business partner)?	
Is this business really solving a problem for customers?	
Can you explain your idea to your grandparents? If not, why?	

6.2 - LOOKING FORWARD

These last five days have been a jump-start on your business idea. Running a business is incredibly hard and isn't something to jump in to lightly. Thinking about the resources and time you'll need and then to be safe adding 50% or more to these numbers (it always takes longer and costs more than you think it will). This will also make you aware the type of partner and skill sets you need to keep an eye out for.

These questions are not binary—some will be positive and some won't. You don't need to commit to running this business for life. Keep in mind the question asked at the end of Day Five—"is it worth spending another Six Days, Six Months or Six Years on this idea?"

What changes do you need to make before taking this further?	
Would running this business make me jump out of bed in the morning? Also consider the answer to this question after working 90 hour work weeks, not seeing your family, and struggling financially. Is it still going to keep you going?	

How much money would I need to test this out further?	
What resources do I have/can draw on to get this going?	
Do you really believe in this idea enough to turn it in to a business?	

What sacrifices/risks are you willing to take to make this happen?	
What would the short and long term goals be for the business—can I see myself doing this for 5-10 years?	
Do I have enough knowledge of this industry to make an impact?	

Do I need a co-founder right now? Will I need one eventually?

Is your idea scaleable? E.g. Consulting is great because it doesn't take many resources to get going, however on the flip side you are effectively trading your time for money—and if you stop working, money will stop coming in. For products, if you are baking every loaf of bread you are making, and you can only make 30 loaves a day, that is your cap. You will not be able to scale without staff. Do you want to take staff on?

Who from the list of people I talked to in Day Five would invest £10, £100 or £1,000 in your idea to give you resources to take this further. Ask them if they would invest—the worst that can happen is they say no.	
What else is relevant to make a decision?	

6.3 - YOUR NEXT STEPS

What are your next steps—do you want to spend more time on your idea and spend 6 days, 6 weeks or 6 months on it? This might seem overwhelming as this step is "ok go do it, or don't".

Instead, plan out the next week. What can you do next? Do you want to spend more time on your prototype, or your online presence? Are there people you want to speak to again? Or maybe you want to take the week off to reflect. The choice is yours. Right now, commit to the one thing you'll do in the next week to take your idea (or not) forward. It might be to do with this idea, it might be to come up with 10 business ideas each day (and really stretch yourself) to keep your creative muscles flexing.

In the next six days I will....

THE BIG QUESTION

Is this worth spending another six days or six weeks on? Why?	
What are the next milestones that you can set? E.g. Sell one loaf of bread at a market (achievable and validates your idea).	

FINAL THOUGHTS

The goal of The Six Day Business is to give you a holistic overview of elements you need to start a business, and get you going on each one. We have just given you a taster of each of the steps—and what they entail.

You might find that you want to spend more time on marketing, or developing a great website, or learning how to sell better. Over the next six weeks you can learn more about each one (there is recommended reading at www.sixday.business/reading) that will allow you to dive deeper.

What we don't want you to do is lose sight of this iterative process of development. Always question what the market wants and needs, and never build something in the hopes that customers will magically appear. As you get better at this process you will be able to iterate more quickly, build what is relevant and make sure there is always a customer for what you are doing. And that is the joy of entrepreneurship—there is always something to learn, build and share with the world.

There is a myth about entrepreneurship—the overnight success. As Lisa Morton said "Some say I'm an overnight success. Well, that was a very long night that lasted about 10 years."

There is a fine balance between listening to other people's advice (like this book) and figuring it out yourself. We aim to provide the structure from which you draw out your own ideas, and come to your own conclusions.

You cannot expect to get everything right the first time, you need to learn, you need to make mistakes, but most importantly you need to start. To this day we are still starting and running businesses and most importantly learning every day. Our own journey, like this book, will continue to evolve as we learn, and build in feedback from others on this journey.

Deciding what to do about an idea that has been bouncing around inside your head for a long time is incredibly difficult. Saying goodbye, or even better 'let's do this,' can be a tough decision to make.

Once we started talking to people about our ideas (whether good or bad) people started appearing who wanted to help, and be a part of what we are doing. This won't happen if you keep an idea inside.

This process was never about the 'silver bullet of success' (and if someone tells you they have that, they're lying). It's never going to be 'yes this idea will work' (unless you have sold out of your service/idea in this week) or 'no it won't' because only the market can decide what will or will not work.

This was about you and your idea, and giving yourself the confidence to take it to market. And you did, and that's incredible—it really is.

As you'll discover, once you start to have ideas, it is tough to stop. This is why it is crucial to continually evaluate your ideas, and then be selective on how to execute on them, and why.

If we could leave you with just two pieces of advice it would be this:

1. Everyone is constantly making things up and pretending to know what they're doing. In reality, there is never going to be a perfect time to do anything—you're not going to be less busy in the future and be ready to start your business. Those who are doing it now probably don't know more than you do, but the difference is they are giving it a shot. The time is now. And remember that everyone started where you are. They thought they could do it so they did. They made it up, they made mistakes, and they persevered.
2. Everything in this world was made by somebody. Made by people just like you. Look around, the chair you're sitting on, the mug you're drinking from—someone conceived it, built it, and sold it. There is no reason that person can't be you.

We are still on the path of entrepreneurship and we know that it will always be something that excites us, motivates us and scares us. Even since we started writing two years ago we learned a huge amount—learnings we are putting in to practice day-by-day. And we know that after we publish this book we will immediately have something else to add (inevitable we know).

We believe that anyone can start a business, whether it is a full time endeavour, or something that keeps you engaged. Whatever it is, it's possible.

We are incredibly happy to have had you with us on this journey, and hope that you can use this process again and again as you continue to come up with, and test, great ideas.

Stay in touch and we look forward to seeing how you do.

ABOUT THE AUTHORS

To find out more about Andrew and Andra visit www.sixday.business/about

Printed in Great Britain
by Amazon